A Little Whale Tale

written by Sam McKendry

illustrated by Carly Castillon

Each and every winter whales take a vacation,
And leave their cold waters for a warm destination.

"This trip is so long," yawned one little whale.
"I must stop for a minute to rest my tired tail!"

But the weary whale fell asleep right away
And found himself alone when he awoke the next day!

"Where did everyone go?" he said all alone.
"I don't know which way they went, or how to get home!"

He searched the blue ocean, but found not one clue
Until he stopped a sea star to see if he knew.

"I have not seen any whales," replied the sea star. "Check with the dolphin. She might know where they are."

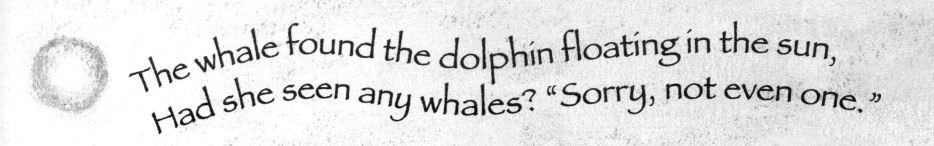

The whale found the dolphin floating in the sun,
Had she seen any whales? "Sorry, not even one."

So the little whale asked, "Which way should I go?"
But the seahorse answered, "I do not know."

He had seen no whales, although he had a suggestion,
"I know who can point you in the right direction."

This was his last chance.
He really was stuck.
The whale asked the octopus,
and hoped for good luck.

Pointing his arms the octopus tried his best, "Have you looked north, south, east, and west?"

The whale swam to the surface for a breath of fresh air. "The sea is so big, they could be anywhere!"

"I will never find them," the whale started to say,
But then off in the distance, he saw water spray!

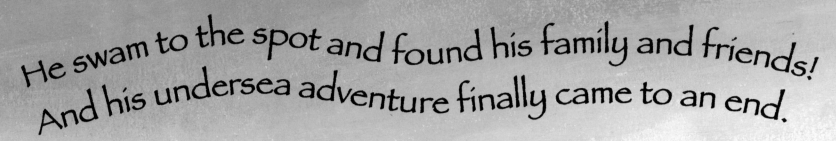

He swam to the spot and found his family and friends!
And his undersea adventure finally came to an end.